How to In Self-Esteem with you!

Jennifer N. Smith

Copyright © 2016 Jennifer N. Smith

All rights reserved.

ISBN: 1539925803

ISBN-13: 978-1539925804

All rights reserved. Without limiting the rights under copyright reserved above, no part of this publication maybe reproduced, stored in or introduced into a retrieval system, or transmitted in any form, or by any means (electronic, mechanical, photocopying, recording or otherwise) without the prior written permission of both the copyright owner and the publisher of this book.

CONTENTS

How to Improve Your Self-Esteem - It all starts with you!

	Introduction	1
1	What is Low Self-Esteem?	2
2	What Causes Low Self-Esteem?	11
3	Activities that you can do to help build self-esteem	17
4	You and Your Health	29
5	Learning how to love yourself	41
6	Fix what you don't like	47
7	Keeping a positive attitude	53
8	Best tips to help improve self-esteem	57
9	Creating an environment that boosts self-esteem	62
10	Always improving	66

Introduction

Your self-esteem affects every area of your life, from your personal relationships to your business success, if your self-esteem is lacking you will find that you face many struggles.

The good news is that you can improve your self-esteem by following a few simple steps which you will learn in this book.

Many people fear that they can never change the way that they feel about themselves, simply accepting their lack of self-esteem. You, however, do not have to be that type of person. This book is going to begin by teaching you exactly what self-esteem is and what creates self-esteem.

We will move on to learning how to build your self-esteem and create the life that you want to live. No longer do you have to wake up wondering what the day will hold or how you will feel throughout the day. You can now by following the information in this book take control of your life.

Chapter 1- What is Low Self-Esteem?

Self-esteem is simply how you feel about yourself. When a person suffers from low self-esteem, they do not feel good about who they are and this can become evident in many different ways. ***Ask yourself, how much you like you.*** If you answer this question honestly, you will be able to determine if you suffer from low self-esteem.

As I stated there are many ways that low self-esteem can make itself evident in a person's life and I want to begin this chapter by talking about how you can tell if you are suffering from low self-esteem.

The first sign that you are lacking in self-esteem that I want to talk about is self-sabotage. This happens when a person has a plan, knows what they need to get done, but sabotages their efforts on their own. You may be sitting there looking at the words on this page and thinking that there is no way that you would sabotage your own efforts, but I want you to take a really good look at your life.

Have you ever had the chance to do something, let's say lose weight for example, and you find yourself sabotaging your own efforts, maybe making extremely heavy, fatty meals for dinner or purchasing foods that you know you should not eat, allowing them to sit in your cabinets and taunt you? Maybe you have had the chance to get everything in your life in order, but instead, <u>allowed yourself to get caught up in a television show instead of taking action, literally sabotaging your entire life</u>.

When you lack self-esteem, you sabotage yourself, because you are trying to confirm to yourself that you can't be successful, that you are not worth it. Subconsciously, you will sabotage the area of your life that you feel the least deserving of, for example, your relationships or your finances.

This type of sabotage can be subtle. Let's imagine that you are trying to start a business on eBay for example. **You have your plan, you have done your research and you know how to make it work. You know that this is going to be it. This is going to be what gets you out of debt, eliminates all of that financial stress and helps you to live the life that you want.**

You put in a ton of hours, making sure that everything is running smoothly, finally you are able to pay your bills with what you earn. Suddenly, you don't put as much effort into your work, even though you know that by working just a bit harder or as hard as you worked in the beginning, you could earn a large amount of money and not have to worry any longer, **<u>you don't do it.</u>**

Why? The reason is because you are sabotaging your own success. You do not feel that you deserve success. Maybe you don't even feel that you even deserve to have nice things or extra money.

The problem however is that you will not just focus on sabotaging one area of your life, once your subconscious is satisfied with sabotaging one area, it will move on to the next area of your life. This happens because your subconscious is looking for more ways to prove yourself correct and to reinforce the way you feel about yourself.

Ask yourself, how much you like you.

If you answer this question honestly, you will be able to determine if you suffer from low self-esteem.

The next way that a lack of self-esteem manifests itself in our lives is that we tend to act as doormats. When a person does not think highly of themselves, they will allow others to treat them poorly and take advantage of them. Often times, a person with low self-esteem will put their own needs on the back burner, focusing on only what other people want or need. If you feel that your only purpose in life is for other people to be their doormat, that is how people are going to treat you.

You see, if you feel that people are always taking advantage of you or lacking respect for you, you have to ask yourself why. If you do not respect yourself, you are not going to expect other people to respect you and you will allow them to talk down to you. You will allow people to scream at you, belittle you, take from you and use you because deep inside, you believe this is what you feel.

It is true, life is full of struggles, sometimes it can feel like problems come at us one after another, however, when you have high self-esteem, you do not let these issues get to you.

You understand that it is simply part of life.

Those who suffer with low self-esteem, however, tend to focus more on the negative parts of life which makes those parts seem so much worse.

When you lack self-esteem you may feel that the entire world is against you, life seems to be one struggle after another and you may feel that there is no point in life. You may feel that life is conspiring against you, that everything goes wrong in your life, that other's treat you poorly because you deserve it and that life is nothing more than a series of struggles.

It is true, life is full of struggles, sometimes it can feel like problems come at us one after another, however, when you have high self-esteem, you do not let these issues get to you. You understand that it is simply part of life. **Those who suffer with low self-esteem, however, tend to focus more on the negative parts of life which makes those parts seem so much worse.**

This often causes a large amount of negative self- talk. People who suffer from low self-esteem not only feel badly about who they are but they talk down to themselves. I am fat. I am stupid. No one will ever love me. I don't have any friends. No one really likes me. I am ugly. These are all examples of negative self-talk and while there are times when everyone's lives when they may feel a bit down about the way they look or their weight, the difference between them and someone that suffers from low self-esteem is that the person with low self-esteem takes part in this negative self-talk <u>all of the time.</u>

the person who is suffering from low self-esteem also is struggling with procrastination. So many people are online right now searching for a way to deal with procrastination and most of them would be surprised to find out that if they dealt with their problems with low self-esteem, they would not have to worry about procrastination. People tend to procrastinate because they doubt their ability to get the task done right.

Let's take for example a person who doubts their abilities to be successful at work. This person will tend to put important tasks off until the very last minute if they complete the task at all. This means that projects get turned on late.

A person with low self-esteem may want to be successful at the things that they attempt in life, however, when it comes down to it, they feel that they are just going to fail and **decide not to even try**. After all, if you know you are going to fail, what is the point in attempting anything? Because of this, a person may begin to believe that they are lazy, they feel even worse about themselves because they never experience what it is like to see success simply because they refuse to try.

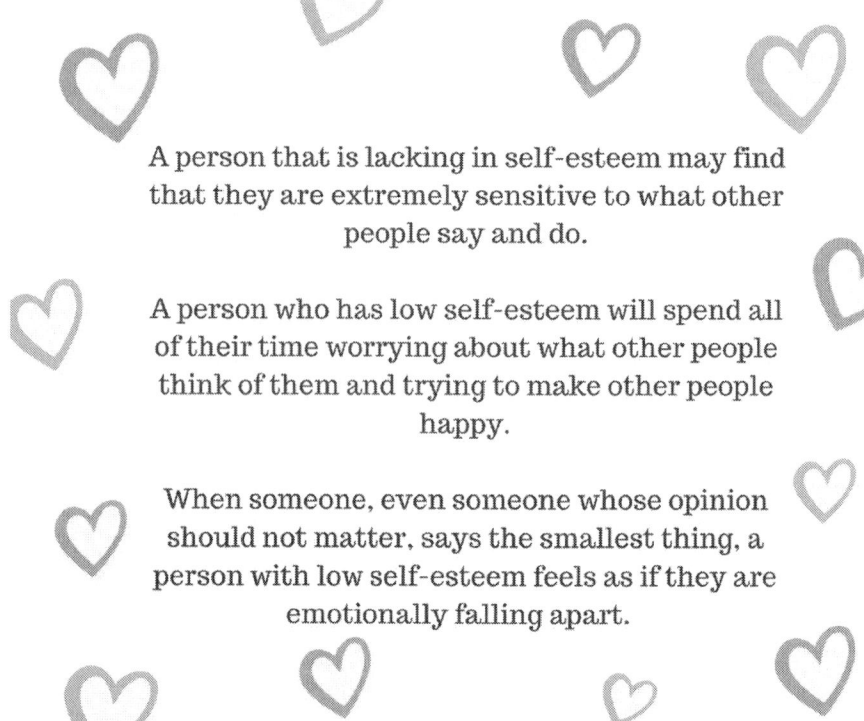

A person that is lacking in self-esteem may find that they are extremely sensitive to what other people say and do.

A person who has low self-esteem will spend all of their time worrying about what other people think of them and trying to make other people happy.

When someone, even someone whose opinion should not matter, says the smallest thing, a person with low self-esteem feels as if they are emotionally falling apart.

<u>Of course, this often means that the person who is suffering from low self-esteem also is struggling with procrastination.</u> So many people are online right now searching for a way to deal with procrastination and most of them would be surprised to find out that if they dealt with their problems with low self-esteem, they would not have to worry about procrastination.

People tend to procrastinate because they doubt their ability to get the task done right. Let's take for example a person who doubts their abilities to be successful at work. This person will tend to put important tasks off until the very last minute if they complete the task at all. This means that projects get turned on late, reports are not filed on time and customers end up angry.

If you are unsure of your social abilities, you may put off going out with your friends or you might even isolate yourself completely. The same is true when it comes to relationships.

Those that suffer from low self-esteem often find themselves feeling embarrassed or suffering from shyness. They may feel that what they want to say is not important enough for anyone to want to listen to them.

This can become so drastic that a person neglects their own health, not going to a doctor because they feel that their life does not matter. It can cause many mental disorders, including the inability to socially interact with anyone. For some people, it gets to the point that they cannot function in normal society, make phone calls or go out in public.

A person that is lacking in self-esteem may find that they are extremely sensitive to what other people say and do.
A person who has low self-esteem will spend all of their time worrying about what other people think of them and trying to make other people happy. **When someone, even someone whose opinion should not matter, says the smallest thing, a person with low self-esteem feels as if they are emotionally falling apart.**

You may also feel very emotional, crying when there really is no reason to cry, suffering from depression when in reality they have nothing to be depressed about. The truth is, if you are suffering from low self-esteem it may be hard for you to recognize at first, <u>but if you really take a good look at your life, it will become quite evident.</u>

Chapter 2- What Causes Low Self-Esteem?

In order to understand how to improve your self-esteem, you have to first learn what causes low self-esteem. **Many people try to blame their parents or their childhood for their lack of self-esteem and while this may be the reason that you suffered from low self-esteem as a child, you really can't blame your parents or childhood once you become an adult.**

The reason is simple. When you become an adult, you move out of your parent's home, and you start taking control of your own life. It is understandable that there might be some things that happened when you were a child that might affect you slightly today, however, if you find that there are issues from your childhood, causing major issues in your adult life, you should seek counseling in order to move past those events.

While there are some things from your childhood, such as

the people around you, that you will still have in your life as an adult, placing the blame on your parents is simply a way to get out of fixing what is really wrong with your life.

I want to begin by talking about the people that you have in your life. Anyone can suffer from low self-esteem, especially if they are living in an environment that feed low self-esteem. People have a lot to do with this environment. **If those that you interact with on a daily basis are not supportive of you or always putting you down, they are only confirming the way that you feel about yourself and you will find that you have less and less self-esteem over time.**

For example, if you are someone that worries about their weight or has had a weight problem in the past, you do not want to surround yourself with people who always tell you that you look like you are gaining weight or who make fun of you because you don't want to eat in front of them. This is only going to feed into your idea of being fat and it is going to cause you to have low self-esteem.

Sometimes, we find that people are only in our lives because they want to bring turmoil into it. As hard as it might be to see or understand right now, these people are victims of the green eyed monster and the only thing that makes them feel better is to make other people feel poorly. They may see you as an easy target because it is obvious that you are suffering from low self-esteem.

Even our most well-meaning friends can be negative influences, telling us that instead of trying something new, we should just stay where we are in life. Usually, they claim that it is because they care about us, that they do not want to see us fail, but we need to ask ourselves if it is really because they do not want to see us succeed.

You need to remember that **like attracts like.** While you have suffered from low self-esteem, you have attracted people into your life that suffer from low self-esteem. You have gained comfort from being around people that are like you, but now that you want

Your physical environment also has a lot to do with your self-esteem. When you look around your home, how does it make you feel?

Do you feel overwhelmed with the clutter? Do you feel inspired or do you feel deflated?

Do you live in such a messy environment that the size of the mess stops you from focusing on anything else?

Do you wish that you had a space that was neat, organized and tidy that you could go to in order to get away from the mess?

to make a change in your life, you have to understand that these people, the ones that suffer from low self-esteem may not be ready to make the same changes in their own lives. This means that they may resist the changes that you are making in your own life, because they know that it will have an effect on them as well. They know that when you make a change in your life, they will either have to change or get left behind.

Your physical environment also has a lot to do with your self-esteem. When you look around your home, how does it make you feel? Do you feel overwhelmed with the clutter? Do you feel inspired or do you feel deflated? Do you live in such a messy environment that the size of the mess stops you from focusing on anything else? Do you wish that you had a space that was neat, organized and tidy that you could go to in order to get away from the mess?

Maybe your environment is too sterile. Maybe the environment is so strict that it makes you feel that you cannot be creative, that you have to adhere to all of the rules and that you cannot express who you really are.

You also need to think about the amount of noise in the environment. Is it too noisy? Maybe it is too quiet.

Look at the room around you, what is it about the room that you feel is stopping you from feeling great about it and yourself. If you look around your home and it makes you feel depressed or ashamed, take some time and decide what it is that you need to do in order to change your environment. We will talk more about how to change your environment later on in this book.

The thought patterns that you have also have a huge impact on your self-esteem. I spoke a bit about negative self-talk earlier in this book, but it goes so much deeper than that. Negative thought patterns can literally make you feel as if the entire world is against you.

Take some time and think about it, how many positive people do you know that suffer from low self-esteem. Now ask yourself the same question about negative people. You might say that the negative people come across as having higher self-esteem, but you have to be able to differentiate between what they are letting people see and what the reality is. You see, if you are around these negative people enough what you will find is that they really do suffer from a lack of self-esteem. You see, while they may spend a lot of time putting other people down, it is because that is the only way that they know how to make themselves feel better about who they are.

Your health can play a huge factor in your self-esteem as well. If you have ever met someone that was sickly most of the time, this is very evident because you can see how because of their illnesses, they do not feel as if they are as good as other people. There are many different ways that health can affect your self-esteem and chronic illness is only one of them. When a person is chronically ill, they may find that as they are trying to make changes in their life, it seems that each time things seem to be going right, or even before the person gets started making the changes, they find themselves falling victim to yet another illness.

When a person does not take care of their body, it can affect their self-esteem and even though they know that there are steps that can be taken to rid their body of the issue that is bothering them, they do not feel motivated to do so. Take, for example, a person that is overweight. Not only is this having a huge impact on their health, but it will affect their self-esteem as well. None of us can avoid looking into a mirror all of the time and when we do, we should like what we see. However, when the way that your body looks begins to affect your self-esteem, you may feel as if you are in a vicious cycle that you cannot get out of.

When self-esteem drops, so does motivation this often means that the person who wants to lose weight and says they will do anything, is not motivated to do the two things that will help them actually lose the weight which is to eat healthily and exercise regularly. Because the person lacks motivation, they will only put on more weight, which means their self-esteem will be lowered and the cycle continues.

If you find that your health is affecting your self-esteem you have to choose to make healthy choices. We will also talk about these healthy choices later on in this book.

The thought patterns that you have also have a huge impact on your self-esteem.

I spoke a bit about negative self-talk earlier in this book, but it goes so much deeper than that. Negative thought patterns can literally make you feel as if the entire world is against you.

Chapter 3- Activities that you can do to help build self-esteem

There are many different things that you can do in order to help build your self-esteem and that is what I want to focus on during this chapter.

I have spoken several times about journals in this book. Journals are going to be hugely beneficial to you. You do not have to keep more than one journal, you can condense all of them into one or you can keep several journals, each serving a different purpose.

In your journal, each morning, while looking in the mirror you should write down three things that you love about yourself. Three compliments that are just for you, for you only. You can have a compliment journal, a gratitude journal (where you write down things you are thankful for), a daily planner type journal where you write down what you want to accomplish each day and what you have accomplished. This could also be referred to as a goal journal. The final type of journal you could have is a typical journal. In this journal, you would write down the events that are taking place in your life, how you feel about the events and so on.

Doing this is going to allow you to look back on your life and see how far you have come. It is amazing sometimes when we keep a journal because as time passes, we really don't see how much we have changed or how much we have accomplished, however, when it is written on paper you can't deny what you have done.

You may also find that when you look back and read about past events that have happened in your life, you are amazed at how much the smallest events bothered you or how you reacted to certain events in your life. **As your self-esteem grows, you will find that you do not let certain things happen in your life any longer.** An example of this might be that in the past you settled in a relationship, allowing your partner to treat you, however they wanted, never feeling as if you deserved anything better. However, at some point, you are going to go back and read your journal, suddenly you will realize that you don't put up with that type of behavior any longer. You will realize that you have grown.

The purpose of this journal or journals is to help you begin practicing self-love and to help you become your own best friend. In your journal, you should be able to express exactly how you feel without worrying about anyone else reading it. It should be something sacred and those around you need to understand that. A journal can contain your innermost thoughts and you should be able to put these on paper while being free from judgment.

When you first begin, you might feel that the journal is

stupid and that you are wasting your time, that is fine and completely normal but stick with it. Imagine that you are a huge barrel, each time you write in your journal, a drop of water is placed in that barrel.

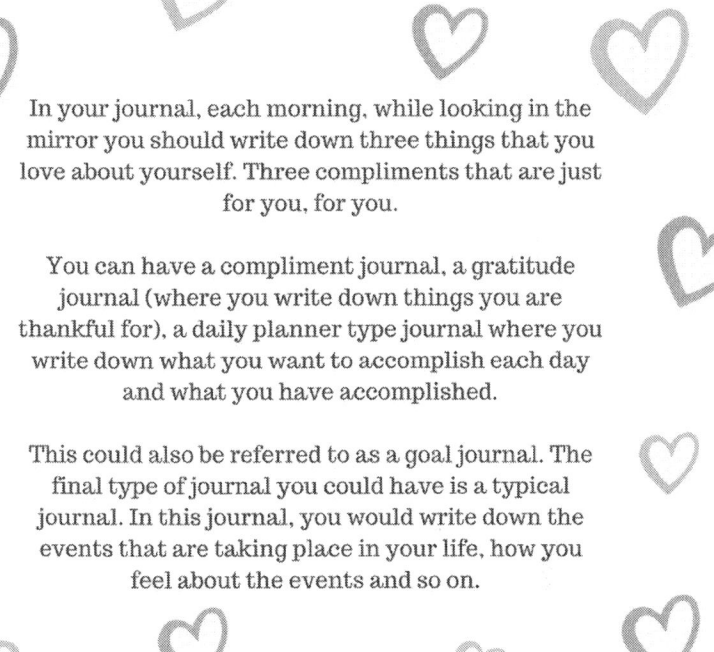

In your journal, each morning, while looking in the mirror you should write down three things that you love about yourself. Three compliments that are just for you, for you.

You can have a compliment journal, a gratitude journal (where you write down things you are thankful for), a daily planner type journal where you write down what you want to accomplish each day and what you have accomplished.

This could also be referred to as a goal journal. The final type of journal you could have is a typical journal. In this journal, you would write down the events that are taking place in your life, how you feel about the events and so on.

Before you know it, the barrel no longer empty but it is full of beautiful life giving water. This water is your self-esteem and right now your barrel is completely empty. This might sound a little strange but trust me, it works.

The next step is to start paying attention to your needs. Often times, we become so focused on other people's needs that we forget about our own. Start with your basic needs, food, water, and shelter. Life can be busy and many times we can forget to eat, which means that later in the day we find ourselves eating large amounts of food that simply is not good for us. Instead of allowing this to happen, we have to make time to eat three meals every day.

People are going to take as much time away from you as you will give them. **If you allow them to take over your meal time, they are going to do it, so set time aside every day for your meals. Water is vital to our health and we all know it, however, it is just another need that we have which we tend to ignore when we are suffering from low self-esteem.** I will talk more about your health in a later chapter because it is so important when it comes to your self-esteem, but you need to know that if you are not providing your body with what it needs, it will not work properly. Many people are surprised to find that they reason they are suffering from depression or other mental illnesses is simply because they are not drinking enough water.

Once you have focused on your basic needs, focus on your other needs. Your need for pleasure. Make sure that you take the time every day to participate in something that you enjoy. It could be something as simple as reading, painting or just spending 30 minutes watching your favorite television show.

Make sure that you are interacting with other people on a daily basis. It is understandable in the world that we are living in that there are some people who want to wall themselves off to the people around them, but I bet you can find at least one person that you can talk to each day. The conversations do not have to be deep meaningful conversations, even the simplest of human contact will work and soon you will find that you are interacting more and more with other people.

When you isolate yourself, you begin to build this fantasy in your mind. You begin to feel that you are completely different than the other people, you may even begin to believe that everyone in the world is perfect and you are the odd man out. Once you begin to interact with other people, you will find that you're not as bad of a person as you thought you were.

Make sure that you are not only nurturing your body, but that you are taking care of your mind as well as your soul. Do things that challenge you. Take part in a spiritual activity, according to your own beliefs. It does not matter what type of activity you take part in but you need to make sure that you are balanced, body, soul and mind because we are made up of all three.

When it comes to taking care of yourself, you can't forget proper hygiene. One thing that happens when a person suffers from low self-esteem is that they stop taking care of their personal hygiene. This can mean that the person stops showering every day, stops shaving, does not brush their teeth, does not floss, does not give themselves manicures or does not fix their hair. **You can suffer from one, all or a mixture of each of these. If you have to create a list of activities that you need to take part in each day, do so.** As you work through the list, put a check by each item. When you take care of your hygiene, you will begin to feel better about who you are. It may seem like a minor step, but you would be amazed at what a difference it makes in the way you feel about yourself.

The way that you dress can also affect your self-esteem so if you want to boost your self-esteem, **you need to start dressing like someone that has high self-esteem.** It is very easy to grab a pair of sweatpants and a T-shirt instead of taking the time to wear a nice looking outfit, but what you are wearing really can change the way that you feel. Find something to wear that you are comfortable in, something that you feel attractive in but also something that you can function in each day. It is perfectly fine to wear sweats and a t-shirt when you are cleaning the house or working in the yard, but when you are going to be around other people you need to make yourself presentable. Not only will you feel better about who you are but you will find that other people treat you differently as well.

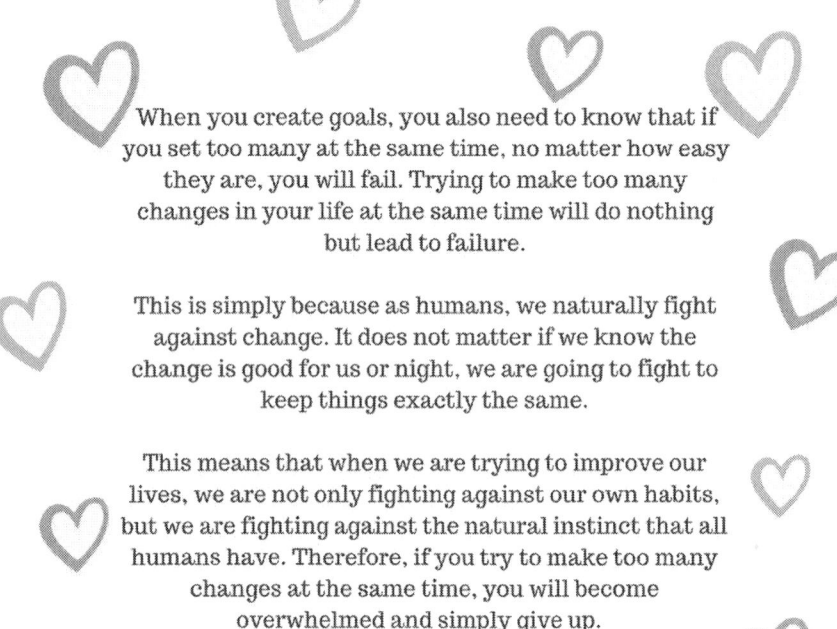

When you create goals, you also need to know that if you set too many at the same time, no matter how easy they are, you will fail. Trying to make too many changes in your life at the same time will do nothing but lead to failure.

This is simply because as humans, we naturally fight against change. It does not matter if we know the change is good for us or night, we are going to fight to keep things exactly the same.

This means that when we are trying to improve our lives, we are not only fighting against our own habits, but we are fighting against the natural instinct that all humans have. Therefore, if you try to make too many changes at the same time, you will become overwhelmed and simply give up.

Spend some time thinking about your abilities. This is a great topic for you to write about in your journal. One of the reasons that many people begin suffering from low self-esteem is because they forget about all of their skills and abilities. They forget about all of the things that make them who they are. **Create a collage or even just a list of all of the things that you are good at and remind yourself of them every day.** If you create a collage, place it somewhere that you will see it daily, such as above your desk.

One reason that many people suffer from low self-esteem is that they set their goals far too high. For example, while a person may want to lose weight, and they may feel very motivated to do so, they try to make too many changes all at the same time. They may decide that they want to exercise for an hour a day. While they may be able to do this for the first day or maybe even two days, what they will find is that their muscles become very sore and they are not able to keep up with the routine. They have set their goals too high, their body simply is not ready for that intense of a workout.

If this person would have **set attainable goals,** they would find that they were able to work out more as time went by. They would be able to stick to their workout routine because they would not feel overwhelmed and they would begin seeing results. This would have provided them with some motivation as well as some self-esteem.

Reaching your goals is going to help you to change the way that you feel about yourself. When you set yourself up for failure, however, you are simply proving to yourself that you can't achieve your goals.

When you create goals, you also need to know that if you set too many at the same time, no matter how easy they are, you will fail. Trying to make too many changes in your life at the same time will do nothing but lead to failure. **This is simply because as humans, we naturally fight against change. It does not matter if we know the change is good for us or night, we are going to fight to keep things exactly the same. This means that when we are trying to improve our lives, we are not only fighting against our own habits, but we are fighting against the natural instinct that all humans have.** Therefore, if you try to make too many changes at the same time, you will become overwhelmed and simply **give up**.

You should set no more than 3 goals at a time and if it is possible one at a time. I know that there are a lot of things that you would like to see change in your life, but there is no possible way for you to change them all at once. Set one large goal, for example, losing 16 pounds in the next two months. Then set one or two smaller goals, such as taking better care of personal hygiene or drinking more water.

When you do this, you will start seeing results faster than you ever imagined, much faster than if you tried to accomplish all of your goals at the same time. When you create a goal, break it down into much smaller goals, that you can work on each day or week. For example, if you want to lose weight, break that goal down. What do you need to do in order to lose weight? Those steps should be goals as well.

Practice using positive affirmations in order to feel better about who you are. There are many guided positive affirmation meditations online that you can use or you can create your own. If you use the guided meditations, you will need to listen to them every day. You can do this at any point during your day, but many people find that doing so as they are falling asleep at night helps the most.

If you want to create your own affirmations, you can write them in your journal. Write positive thoughts about yourself, such as:

I am beautiful.

I am smart.

I am strong.

I am healthy.

I am loved.

And so on. Try to write at least 10 of these affirmations every night. If you are having a hard time coming up with affirmations, come up with 10 and every night before you go to bed, read them to yourself. Every morning when you wake up, read them again and when you are starting to feel poorly about yourself, read them.

When you are writing an affirmation, you need to focus on the areas of your life that you feel you are struggling with the most. For example, if you find that you are procrastinating while you are working, write an affirmation stating that you are a productive person.

This may seem as if you are lying to yourself, but what happens is that these affirmations almost rewire the way that your brain works. Instead of believing that you are a procrastinator, you will begin believing that you are a very productive person.

When this happens, you will change your actions in order to prove yourself right, just the same as you would if you were using negative self-talk.

When you are writing these affirmations, you need to make sure that you are only using positive words. Negative words such as can't, no, never and so forth should not be used in affirmations. For example, instead of saying, "I will never eat fast food again," you will say, "I choose to eat healthy foods because I deserve to have a healthy body." Remove the negative and replace it with something positive.

Use affirmations every day for at least 90 days. The more open to the process you are, the sooner they will begin to work. Many times, these affirmations will begin working in as little as a week. For some people it can take up to a month before they see changes, but it is important for you to continue using the affirmations even after you begin seeing results. You do not want to fall back into your old way of thinking.

Find a hobby that you enjoy that you can do on your own. It does not have to be something complex, learning how to crochet, write a book, garden or do whatever you enjoy, but make sure that you do not have to rely on anyone else to help you with the hobby. People tend to forget that they do need to take time to be alone. We may feel that we are technically alone while we are at work, sitting at our desks, focusing on our work, but the truth is, you have to spend time alone doing something that you enjoy. When you spend time alone, doing what you enjoy, you will find that you are recharged, that you feel better about yourself and that minor issues do not get to you as much as they used to. This hobby needs to be something that does not feel like just another chore because if it feels like a chore, you are not going to enjoy doing it and it is not going to help you relax.

Finally, it is important for you to change the way that you think. Instead of allowing yourself to focus on the negative all of the time, change your negative thoughts into positive thoughts. For example, if you find yourself thinking that you cannot do something, change that thought as soon as you notice it and tell yourself that there is nothing that you cannot do. If you find yourself thinking that you are a loser, remind yourself of all of the things that you have accomplished in your life. Remind yourself that you are a successful person, changing the negative thought into a positive one.

Spend some time thinking about the life that you want, while you are doing this, visualize yourself living that life. Visualize yourself being happy, being successful and so on. **Don't just think of yourself living this life, but feel the feelings that you would have if you were living the life that you want to live. What would be different from your life right now?**

When you spend time visualizing, you will find that your goals become much clearer, that you can quickly break down the steps that you need to take in order to reach those goals and you will be able to easily remind yourself that you can reach those goals.

Chapter 4- You and Your Health

I have stated several times in this book that your health plays a huge factor on your self-esteem. I can tell you from personal experience that this is true. Growing up, I was known as the weakling in the family. Very pale, always sick and this continued into adulthood. Many times I would find myself wondering what I had done in order to deserve this. Surely, I wasn't worthy of a good life because if I was, I would not be sick all of the time.

One day, in my 20's it clicked. I am in charge of my own health. While I might not have had much say in my health as a child, I was an adult and it was time for me to begin making the changes that needed to be made.

If you have ever been very healthy and then found yourself extremely unhealthy you know how it can affect the way that you feel about yourself. That is why I wanted to dedicate an entire chapter to this topic. What makes this dangerous is that low self-esteem is going to affect your health as well. This is a vicious circle that has to be broken if you want to get healthy and have a healthy level of self-esteem.

Not only does low self-esteem affect your physical health, but it affects your mental health as well. When a person is suffering from low self-esteem, they will usually find that they are dealing with depression and anger. Of course, both anger and depression can affect your physical health, leaving you completely exhausted and stressed. On top of this, anger and depression can make you feel as if you are a bad person or as if you have no value. This means that your self-esteem lowers and all of the effects become much worse.

This means that you have to take the time to improve your health if you ever want to increase your self-esteem and live the life that you want to live. This is why I have focused so much on health and weight in this book.

We all know that it can seem almost impossible to take the time to live a healthy lifestyle in the world that we live in today. We are very busy people, we have so many responsibilities that at times it seems that we cannot handle all of them and when we think about changing our entire lifestyle in order to live healthier, it can be very overwhelming, however, there are some very simple changes that you can make in your life that will put you on the road to better health while not taking up a lot of your time.

The first thing that you will want to focus on is nutrition. **The reason for this is because if you do not give your body the nutrients that it needs, your body is not going to be able to function properly.** This means that you will feel exhausted, you will suffer from mental disorders, you will feel depressed and all of your efforts to overcome a lack of self-confidence will be in vain.

One of the best things that you can do for your body is to cut out all fast food and start eating real food. I will be the first to admit that there are many nights when you do not feel like cooking, nights when you don't have time to cook a meal from scratch. **There are alternatives to fast food on these nights, though. One thing that I like to do is to make what is called freezer meals once a month. These are simply homemade meals that you place in a freezer bag, pop in the crockpot in the morning or in the oven when you get home from work and you don't have to worry about spending a lot of time in the kitchen.**

You can make a few meals, for those nights that you are too busy cooking or you can make an entire month's worth of meals in just a few hours. In fact, it takes about four hours for me to make a month's worth of meals and place them in the freezer. Now, these four hours of cooking only happens once a month and it saves me a ton of time during the rest of the month. Not only does it save me a ton of time, help ensure that my family is eating healthy home cooked meals every night. What you are trying to do is to prepare healthy, tasty meals with as little work as possible while spending as little time at the grocery store as possible.

Even if you do not want to make freezer meals, using your crockpot is a great way to ensure that you have the healthy food that your body needs. There are many soups and stews that you can make in a crockpot and the great news is that there is so much more than soups and stews that can be made in the crockpot. It is a very great feeling when you come home after a long day at work and your dinner is already prepared for you.

Of course, no one wants to eat meals out of a crockpot all of the time, so it is also a great idea for you to learn how to make a few three ingredient meals, especially for the weekends when you have a bit more time to spend in the kitchen.

If you do not know how to cook, this is something that you should really consider learning because not only will it allow you to prepare healthy meals at home but it provides you with a sense of pride. When you sit down at the dinner table and watch your family enjoying the food that you have made for them, it will help to boost your self-esteem. Soon you will realize that you can make amazing meals and if you can do that, you can do anything.

Eliminating processed food is also a great idea when it comes to becoming a healthier person. Of course, you are not going to be able to eliminate all processed foods from your diet, there will be some foods that you need such a cheese and milk but there are also many foods that your body does not need such as cookies, chips, candy, pop and juice. Processed foods are packed full of sugar, even when they claim to have reduced fat, they are still packed with sugar because sugar is technically fat free.

You will be amazed at how different you feel when you eliminate as much processed food from your diet as possible. You will become more energetic, you will feel happier and your mind will feel clearer than ever.

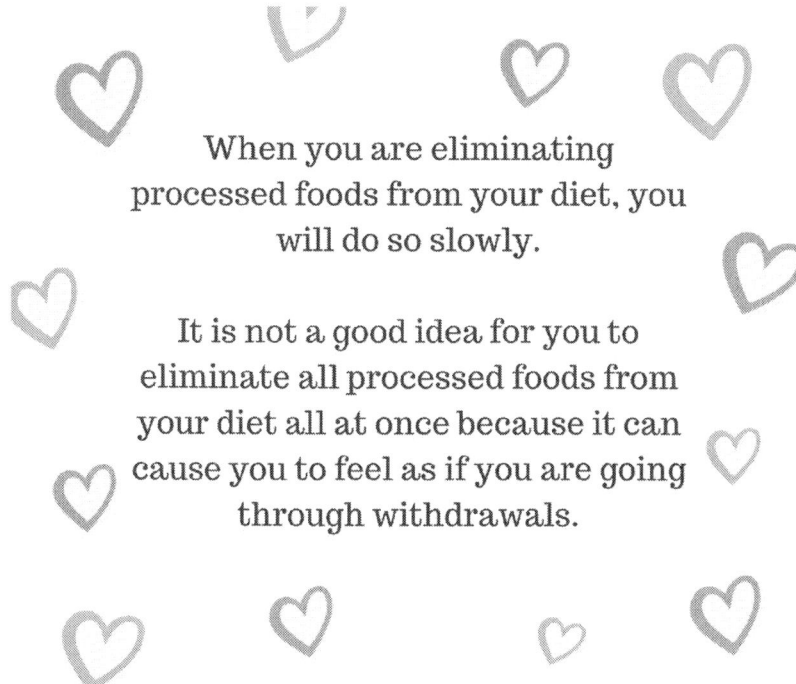

When you are eliminating processed foods from your diet, you will do so slowly.

It is not a good idea for you to eliminate all processed foods from your diet all at once because it can cause you to feel as if you are going through withdrawals.

When you are eliminating processed foods from your diet, you will do so slowly. It is not a good idea for you to eliminate all processed foods from your diet all at once because it can cause you to feel as if you are going through withdrawals. You see, sugar is like a drug, your body has become very addicted to it, that is why you have cravings and feel sick when you cannot get the sugar that your body is craving. If you eliminate all of the processed foods from your diet all at once, you are going to go through extreme withdrawals. Your body is going to crave sugar, you are going to feel sick, weak and can even suffer from headaches. This is simply your body trying to detox from the sugar.

Instead of going through all of this, look at the foods that you eat and try to come up with healthy alternatives. For example, if you drink a lot of soda, choose water instead.

Juice, sports drinks or diet soda is not a good option because they are all processed, sugary drinks that are very bad for you. Diet soda of course is not a sugary drink, but the sugar alternative that is used, has been linked to many diseases including mental disorders, cancer and obesity. Make one or two changes at a time, removing the bad foods from your diet and replacing them with healthy alternatives. Soon you will find

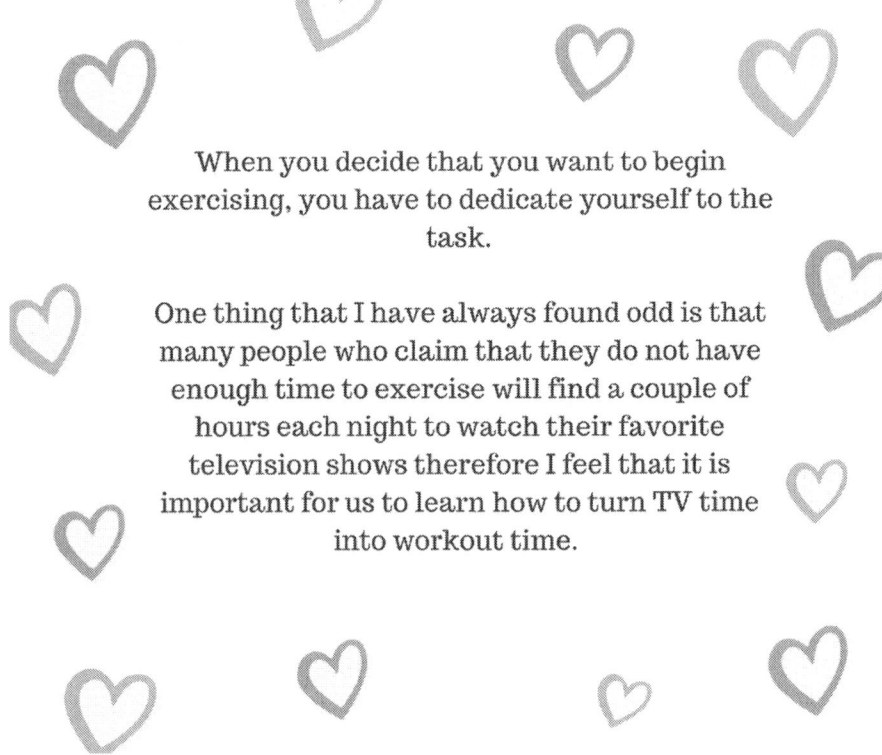

> When you decide that you want to begin exercising, you have to dedicate yourself to the task.
>
> One thing that I have always found odd is that many people who claim that they do not have enough time to exercise will find a couple of hours each night to watch their favorite television shows therefore I feel that it is important for us to learn how to turn TV time into workout time.

that you are craving more and more vegetables, fruits and healthy foods while your cravings for the processed food is eliminated.

The next thing that I want to talk about when it comes to your health is exercise. **Most of the jobs that we have today consist of sitting at a desk for the majority of**

the day. After we sit at our desks, we come home and sit down to dinner, then we sit down to watch television before going to bed. That leads to a lot of inactivity in our lives. This means that many people are gaining weight, even when they are eating healthy foods, they find that the weight just keeps piling on and they cannot understand why.

This is why exercise is so important. You see, our bodies were created to move. When humans first came into existence, they did not stay in the same area for a long time, they were hunters and gatherers, even exercising just to find the food that would provide them with the energy to find more food. Obesity did not become a problem in our world until we stopped exercising.

Many people tell themselves that they are going to start exercising, they even purchase exercise equipment, placing it in their living room or bedroom, having every intention of using it. What happens, however, is that the exercise equipment often becomes a catch all, clothes are hung over it, items are piled on top of it and it is never used for fitness.

When you decide that you want to begin exercising, you have to dedicate yourself to the task. One thing that I have always found odd is that many people who claim that they do not have enough time to exercise will find a couple of hours each night to watch their favorite television shows therefore I feel that it is important for us to learn how to turn TV time into workout time. This does not mean that you cannot watch your favorite television shows. If you are one of those people who purchased some exercise equipment, such as a stationary bike, you can use the equipment while watching your favorite show.

You will be surprised at how quick the time goes by if you exercise while watching television. If you do not have any equipment, create a workout plan that you can do on the floor in front of the television. Do some sit ups, push-ups, yoga poses, or whatever exercise you like while you are watching television.

You can also turn exercise time into family time as well. After dinner, do your regular evening clean up, then take your family for a walk. Enjoy being outside, go for a hike or just play ball in the front yard. You do not have to spend a ton of time in the evening walking or playing, 30 minutes is fine, but what you will find is that not only is your health going to benefit but your families will as well. On top of this, you will be creating memories for your children. Your children will look back on the time that you spent together one day and it will bring them happiness. It will also ensure that they know how to have family time with their own children.

Mix things up. You don't want to have to force yourself to do your workout routine every day because it has become so boring to you. The way to avoid this is to change things up on a regular basis. Don't just ride your bike, but walk, lift weights, play in the yard or go for a long hike. In the summer, swim if that is something you enjoy.

The good news is that you don't have to force yourself to exercise a lot each day. Thirty minutes a day is great as long as you are continuing to be active the rest of the day. You have to remember that a body in motion tends to stay in motion and a body at rest tends to stay at rest. Therefore, don't look around your house and complain that nothing ever gets done as you relax in your recliner, **instead, keep moving. Get as much done as you can each day instead of wasting your time.**

The fact is, you only get one life and you don't want to waste it doing nothing.

It is understandable that there are going to be times when you want to do nothing more than relax and that is fine as long as it does not happen on a regular basis. What you will find if you are active the majority of your waking hours is that you will have more energy, be able to get more done, feel better about who you are, lose weight faster and you are going to sleep better at night.

Sleep is the next thing that I want to talk about. So many people that are overweight struggle with getting enough sleep. The reason for this is simply because their body has not used up enough energy to feel as if it needs a lot of sleep. I talk to many overweight people on a regular basis that complain about their body hurting when they go to bed or simply not being able to fall asleep. What do I tell them? I let them know that this is happening because they are not getting enough exercise.

If you find that you are unable to sleep at night, you need to look at what is happening during the day. First, you need to ask yourself if you are sleeping during the day. If you are taking a lot of naps during the day, you need to stop. You are going to have to break the habit of sleeping during the day and get into the habit of sleeping at night.

I have spoken to many people who will sleep all day long then not understand why they cannot fall asleep at night, telling me that they never get any sleep. The truth is that they are getting a lot of sleep, in fact, that is all they are focusing on in life but they are not getting restful sleep. Our bodies were made to sleep at night, they were made to sleep when it is dark outside not when the sun is shining through the windows.

The second thing that you need to look at if you are not getting enough sleep, is the amount of exercise you are getting. If you are not getting any exercise, your body is not going to be tired and you are not going to need the same amount of sleep as someone who is very active. Even though mentally you may feel drained, your body is not tired.

The third thing that you need to think about is the amount of sleep that you think you need. If you are only sleeping three hours a night, you are going to be tired, your body is not going to function properly, chances are that you will suffer from low self-esteem, depression and other mental disorders. The truth is, a very active person will need between 8-9 hours of sleep each night. A person that is not very active will only need about 6 hours of sleep a night.

If you are very tired, but know that you are getting more than enough sleep, you need to pay attention to what is going on. You see, if you are getting too much sleep, you can become overly exhausted as well. Try cutting back on the amount of sleep you are getting, waking up earlier, going to bed later and avoiding naps.

While getting enough sleep is important to your body, it is just as important that you ensure you are not sleeping too much.

Finally, to finish up this chapter I want to talk about water. It amazes me how few people drink water. Instead of filling their body with a live giving liquid, they want to instead fill it with poison, choosing soda, juices, or sports drinks.

Our bodies are made up of 70 percent water and as we go about our day our bodies lose water. Because of this, it is vital to our health that we replenish that water by drinking at least 64 ounces of water each day. This may seem almost impossible, but it really is not that difficult. When you think about drinking 4-16 ounce glasses of water each day it is not that hard. You can start out your day by drinking a glass of water instead of drinking a cup of coffee. Then have a glass of water with your breakfast instead of juice. Remember that juice is not going to provide you with the same nutrients as fruit, so it is best to eliminate it from your diet. Instead of having juice at breakfast, **<u>drink a glass of water and have a piece of fruit.</u>**

Have another glass of water at lunch as well as one at dinner. If you are very dehydrated and trying to rehydrate yourself, it is also a good idea for you to sip on a glass or two of water throughout the day.

It is easy to tell how hydrated you are by the color of your urine. If your urine is not clear, then that means that you are dehydrated to some extent. If your urine is dark yellow or orange, it is vital that you rehydrate yourself because this is a sign that you are extremely dehydrated.

Dehydration causes so many health issues, both physically and mentally and that is why it is vital for you to ensure you are getting enough water. If you want to increase your self-esteem, you have to be determined to take care of your body.

Chapter 5- Learning how to love yourself

If you cannot love yourself, there is no way that anyone else will ever truly be able to love you. The question is, though, how do you begin loving yourself? Many people will tell you to love yourself, get into a relationship with yourself, spend time figuring out who you really are, however, **they never tell us how we are supposed to do this.**

As I traveled on my own path to self-love, I learned many things, what does work as well as what does not and that is what I want to share with you in this chapter.

<u>The first thing that you have to do if you want to love yourself is to stop comparing yourself to others.</u> It is something that many of us do much more often than we realized. We compare the way that we look to the way we perceive others. When we look in the mirror, we tend to focus on our flaws. However, when we look at other people we tend to look past their flaws and only notice how beautiful they are. What we do not see though, is what they look like when they wake up in the morning. We do not see their stretch marks, their fat rolls or their cellulite. One thing that you have to remember is that while you are busy looking at other people, wishing that you were as beautiful as they are, someone is looking at you thinking the same thing.

There is no reason for you to ever compare the way that you look to the way that other people look because every human has something beautiful about them. You should also not compare your job, your achievements, your home or anything about yourself to other people. Yes, there is always going to be someone out there that earns more than you, that is smarter than you or that has better things that you do. None of this matters. **You have to learn to be happy with what you have and who you are, <u>only then will you truly be able to love yourself.</u>**

While it is important for you to be healthy, you cannot focus solely on your weight. One thing that I personally had to learn was that weight is not something that matters. While I have always weighed more than most people, I have also been thin. I am a very muscular person, but when I would step on the scale, all I would see was a number that I hated. I had to learn just as you have to that the number on the scale does not measure your value and if you want to lose fat, you do have options, **however, you should not focus on weight, instead, focus on your health.**

Exercise simply because you know that it will make you feel good, it will make you sleep better, and it is good for your body. **Do not exercise simply because you want to lose weight. While it is important for you to feel good about your body, what you will find is that when you exercise, you will feel much better about yourself, you will begin to feel pride and you will begin to love who you are.**

When it comes to your job, it can make you or break you and I am not talking about monetarily. If you do not love what you do, you are not going to be happy with your life,

The first thing that you have to do if you want to love yourself is to stop comparing yourself to others. It is something that many of us do much more often than we realized.

We compare the way that we look to the way we perceive others. When we look in the mirror, we tend to focus on our flaws. However, when we look at other people we tend to look past their flaws and only notice how beautiful they are.

you are not going to be proud of yourself, you are not going to be able to love yourself because you are always going to be dreading going to work. Instead, find something that you are good at, something that you enjoy and don't let money determine what you are going to spend the rest of your life doing. If you enjoy working with children, find a job that you enjoy, where you can work with children. If you enjoy writing, find a job that will allow you to write and so on. What you will find when you have a job that you enjoy, one that **you are proud of doing is that you are more successful than when you were working a job that you did not enjoy.**

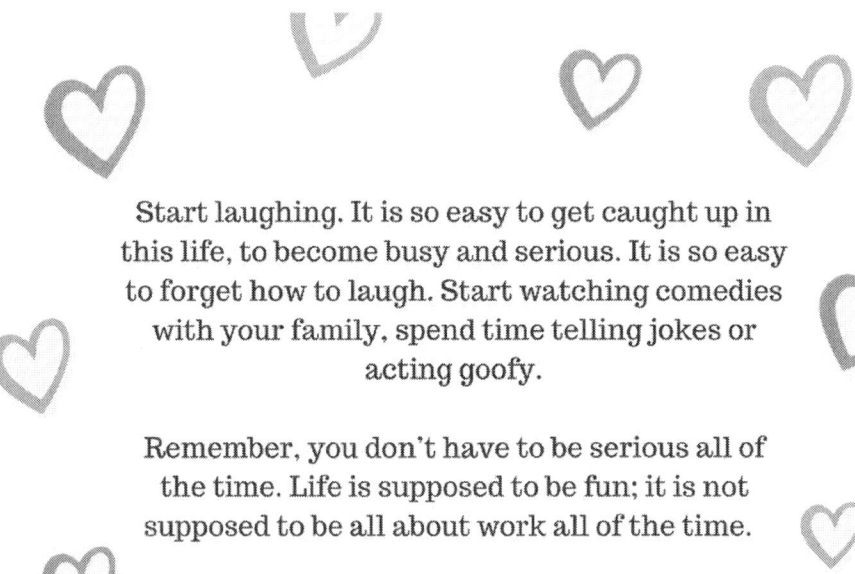

Start laughing. It is so easy to get caught up in this life, to become busy and serious. It is so easy to forget how to laugh. Start watching comedies with your family, spend time telling jokes or acting goofy.

Remember, you don't have to be serious all of the time. Life is supposed to be fun; it is not supposed to be all about work all of the time.

Make sure that you are spending time alone. You do not have to spend every Friday night out with your friends. Instead, make a date with yourself. Make some food that you enjoy, pick out a few movies, pamper yourself with a bubble bath, manicure and then curl up on the couch with a cozy blanket and watch those movies. You should never feel bad for not going out with your friends. You have to take time for yourself, time to relax and just enjoy being alone.

Spend time reading, not just self-help books but fiction books. Get lost in a world that does not exist. Do you remember how much you loved to read when you were younger? Find that love for reading again and plan time to do it as often as possible.

It is so important for you to spend time outside as well. We have become people who have forgotten that there is a world outside of your homes and outside of technology. Take time to get outside, enjoy the sun and when you just can't get outside, open up the shades or open the windows letting in fresh air.

Resolve issues that you have with family and friends. If you really want to love yourself, you have to learn how to let things from the past go.

Let people who have hurt you know that you forgive them, **but that does not mean that you should allow people to walk all over you in the future. Stand up for yourself if you feel that someone is not treating you the way that you deserve to be treated <u>but do so in a mature and respectful way.</u>**

Take the time to care about the way that you look. This does not mean that you have to be vain or that you have to walk around with your nose stuck in the air thinking you are more beautiful than any other person. It simply means that you wear clean clothes that are free of stains or holes, that you brush your hair, take care of your teeth and show the world that you love who you are.

Start laughing. It is so easy to get caught up in this life, to become busy and serious. It is so easy to forget how to laugh. Start watching comedies with your family, spend time telling jokes or acting goofy. Remember, you don't have to be serious all of the time. Life is supposed to be fun; it is not supposed to be all about work all of the time.

Finally, realize that you are never going to be able to please everyone, you are not going to be able to make everyone like you, and you are not going to enjoy spending time with every single person that you meet. The good news is that this is okay. You don't have to worry about making anyone else happy, or making anyone like you.

You never have to worry about forcing yourself to like anyone else. Just be yourself and the right people will come into your life.

Chapter 6- Fix what you don't like

We all have things in our lives that we do not like. There are things about ourselves that we don't like, things about our homes, our finances and pretty much every area of our lives. When there are a lot of things in our lives that we do not like, we end up focusing on them and that can lead to low self-esteem.

What are we supposed to do when there are things in our lives that we do not like? You are doing exactly what you are supposed to be doing right now. Work to change it.

The first thing that I want you to do is to look at the things about you and your life that you do like. Chances are that you are going to find that the things that you do like are things that you have personally chosen for your life.

The next thing I want you to do is to ask yourself whose life are you actually living? Are you living the life that you planned for yourself? The life that you want to live? Or are you living the life that someone else wants you to live?

One of the main reasons that people do not like different parts of their life or their entire life is because they are not following the path that they want to follow. Instead, a person that is unhappy with their life is usually following a path that has been planned out by someone else.

Take for example, a woman that never wanted to be married. She may find that she is very unhappy with her life because she has been pushed for so long by those that she loves to get married. She forces herself to date, even though she has no interest in it, but instead she wants to spend her life focusing on her own success. This woman is living her life to please other people and no matter how hard she tries, as long as she continues to do this, she will never find happiness nor will she feel good about herself.

I want you to take a few moments and look at your life. Do you feel that you are living the life that you want to live or do you feel that you are living a life that has been forced on you by others?

What do you need to change so that you can feel that you are living the life that you want to live? One thing that people forget is that they do not have to conform to what the rest of the world thinks of as normal.

Take, for instance, the person that works from home, running their own business. When a person works from home, they do not have to conform to regular work hours, they can work when they want to work, how much they want to work and often times they can earn as much as they want to earn. On the other hand, a person that works a 'regular' job has to work a certain number of hours each week, they have to punch in and out, they have to do exactly what their boss wants them to and they have no choice when it comes to how much they will earn.

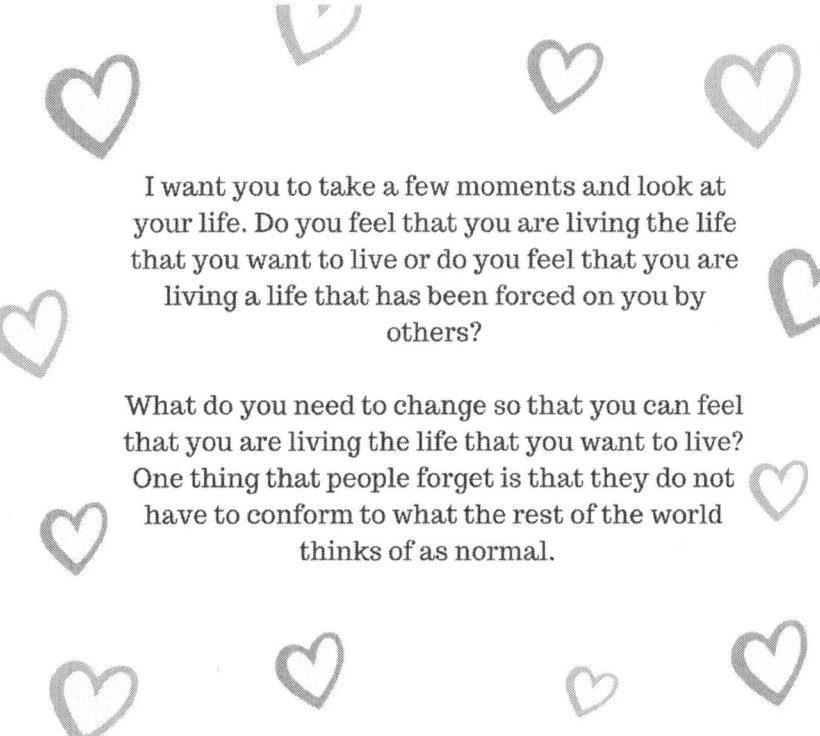

I want you to take a few moments and look at your life. Do you feel that you are living the life that you want to live or do you feel that you are living a life that has been forced on you by others?

What do you need to change so that you can feel that you are living the life that you want to live? One thing that people forget is that they do not have to conform to what the rest of the world thinks of as normal.

When people who have never experienced working from home look at this person who does it for a living, they may perceive it as odd because it is not the norm, but if that is what makes the person happy, then that is all that really matters. You see, we live in a world today where you don't have to conform to what other people think is normal, you can be who you want to be and not care what anyone thinks about it.

This means that no matter who has influenced your life in the past, you don't have to continue allowing them to influence it any longer. Live the life that is going to make you happy and don't let anyone make you feel bad for doing so.

The next question that you need to ask yourself is if you are always looking at the negative when it comes to your life. Are you always listening to that inner voice that is critical of everything that you do and everything that happens in your life? Of course, this voice can be beneficial when we know that we are not living our life to the fullest, however, we need to learn that this voice can cause damage as well.

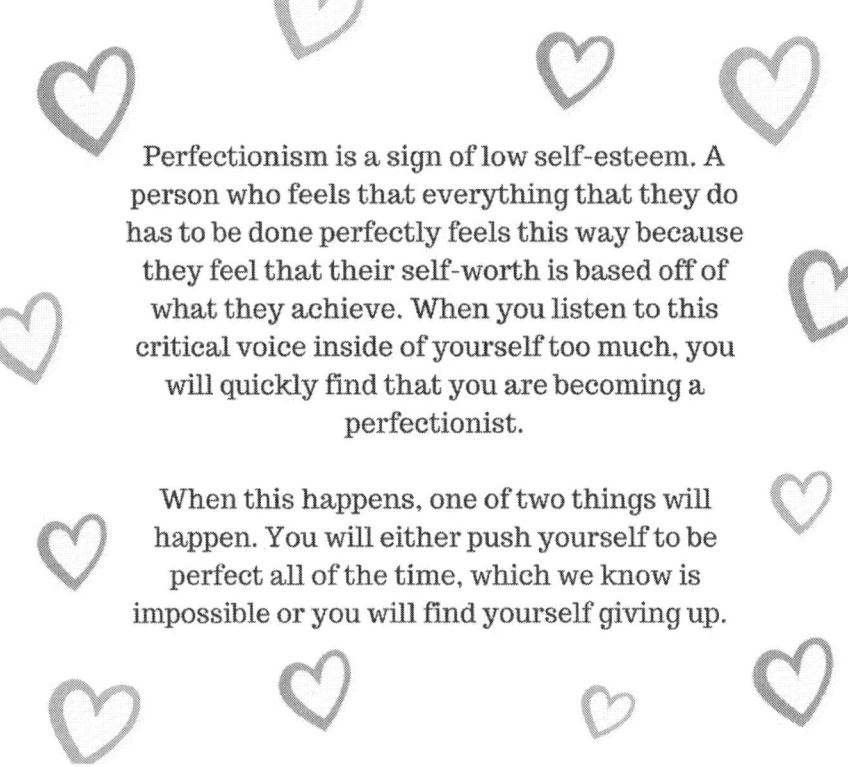

Perfectionism is a sign of low self-esteem. A person who feels that everything that they do has to be done perfectly feels this way because they feel that their self-worth is based off of what they achieve. When you listen to this critical voice inside of yourself too much, you will quickly find that you are becoming a perfectionist.

When this happens, one of two things will happen. You will either push yourself to be perfect all of the time, which we know is impossible or you will find yourself giving up.

The critical voice inside of you is something that we all need because it tells us that we could do more, we

could be more successful and we could live a better life. However, it has to be kept under control because it can also cause you to become a perfectionist.

<u>Perfectionism is a sign of low self-esteem.</u> A person who feels that everything that they do has to be done perfectly feels this way because they feel that their self-worth is based off of what they achieve. When you listen to this critical voice inside of yourself too much, you will quickly find that you are becoming a perfectionist. When this happens, one of two things will happen. **<u>You will either push yourself to be perfect all of the time, which we know is impossible or you will find yourself giving up.</u>**

It is vital that we take control of this inner critic. When you find yourself being critical of yourself, for example, telling yourself that you did not accomplish enough, remind yourself of all that you did accomplish. If you find that the voice is right, create a plan to ensure that you do what you need to do the following day.

One great way for you to change your life is to practice what is called mindfulness. In short, mindfulness means that you do not focus on the past and you do not worry about the future, but you fully focus on what is happening right now. For example, if you are taking a shower, you fully focus on that shower. You feel the water, you experience the smells of the soaps you are using and you remind yourself that never in your life have you before, right this instant taken this bath and had this experience.

This goes for everything that you do every single day. This will help not only to reduce the stress in your life, but it will help you to stay focused on what is going on in your life in the present moment.

Another great way for you to make changes in your life is like I said at the beginning of this chapter, simply continue doing what you are doing. Right now, you are taking the time out of your life to read a self-help book. You are taking the steps that you need to take in order to change something about yourself or your life that you do not like. There are thousands of self-help books out there that can help you with any area of your life.

No matter what it is that you do not like about your life, the good news is that you can change it. You are in control of your life. You are in control of what happens in your life and you are in control of your own happiness.

Chapter 7- Keeping a positive attitude

I have stated several times in this book how important it is for you to keep a positive attitude if you want to improve your self-esteem. I have talked about positive affirmations as well as meditation, but I want to go into depth a bit more and talk about how important it is for you to keep a positive attitude if you want to improve your self-esteem.

The attitude that you have is going to be what determines the type of life that you have. It is going to determine your success, what happens in your relationships, and how happy you are overall. Your attitude is going to be determined by your mental diet. **What is your mental diet?** Your mental diet is going to be everything that you put into your mind. The thoughts that you think, the shows that you watch, the books that you read and the conversations that you have.

If you are always putting negative in, negative is what is going to come out in your attitude. On the other hand, if you are always feeding your mind positivity, positivity is what is going to come out as your attitude.

This means that you have to make the decision to take complete control of your mind instead of letting your mind take control of you. You have to choose to eliminate all of the negative emotions from your mind as well as the negative thoughts. You have to let the past go, no matter how much pain you have dealt with and focus only on what is going on right now. You have to vow to become 100 percent positive.

You can begin changing your attitude by using positive affirmations just as we discussed in previous chapters, use visualization, and meditation. There are many other ways for you to change your attitude from negative to positive.

Take a look at the television shows that you watch on a regular basis. Is what you are watching of a negative tone? For example, do you spend the majority of your time watching horror or other negative genre? What about the music that you listen to? Is it negative music or is it uplifting and positive? What about the books that you read?

Look at everything that you put into your mind and change it to positive instead of negative. Instead of watching negative television shows, watching something that is uplifting. Instead of listening to angry or sad music, listen to something that makes you feel good or makes you happy. When you read a book, read an inspirational book, one that makes you feel motivated instead of one that makes you break down and cry.

The next thing that you need to look at is the type of people that you have in your life. We all have people in our lives that are negative and if you begin paying close attention, what you will find is that when you are around these type of people, you become very negative as well. Once you realize this, you will understand why it is so important for you to distance yourself from these types of people.

> If you are always putting negative in, negative is what is going to come out in your attitude.
>
> On the other hand, if you are always feeding your mind positivity, positivity is what is going to come out as your attitude.

If a parent or close loved one is a negative person, you may want to talk to them about their attitude, show them that you are concerned and ask that they try to not be so negative when they are around you. If you find yourself becoming negative while you are around them, find a space to clear your mind and focus on something positive.

Do not let someone else's negative attitude determine how you feel or behave.

Again, it is vital that you focus on your health if you want to be a positive person. It is said that fatigue can make a failure out of anyone and that is true. If you are not giving your body what it needs, when it comes to food, water, exercise, and sleep, how can you expect your body to work properly for you?

You need to make sure that you are not pushing yourself too hard or expecting too much of yourself. If you do push yourself too hard, you are going to find that you are sick more often, that you are getting less and less done and that you feel poorly about yourself.

Finally, it is important that you expect positive things to happen. This means that what you focus on the most is what you attract to your life. Therefore, if you are focusing on only negative things and expecting only negative things to happen, that is what you are going to attract into your life, however, <u>if you are focusing on positive things and expecting only positive things to happen in your life, that is what you will attract into your life.</u>

Living with a positive attitude is not always easy, but it does get easier with time and the payoff is enormous.

Your attitude affects every area of your life so why not make sure that it affects it positively?

Chapter 8- Best tips to help improve self-esteem

I have talked about many different ways for you to improve your self-esteem throughout this book, but I want to touch on a few more tips that you can use in this chapter.

1. **Set your intention for the day.** Before you ever step foot out of your bed in the morning, plan the type of day that you are going to have. Adjust your attitude and get in a good mood. Plan to be productive, positive and plan on making your day exactly what you want of it. As your day progresses, look for ways to help you create the day that you want.

2. **Make sure that you begin your day with a plan.** Always sit down the night before and create a plan for what you want to get done the next day. Make sure that you have enough time to get everything done and that you are not over-scheduling yourself. When you do this, you will know exactly what you need to accomplish as soon as your day begins and will not find yourself wondering what you are supposed to be

doing. You will also find that you feel a sense of pride when you accomplish, all that you have set your mind to.

3. **Always take the time to celebrate your successes.** You do not have to do anything huge, reward yourself with a nice bubble bath when you have accomplished all of your goals for the day or a manicure, or even an episode of your favorite television show. Just make sure that what you reward yourself does not set you back on any of your other goals. For example, if you want to lose 60 pounds, do not reward yourself with cupcakes every time you complete a goal.

4. **Practice gratitude.** Be grateful for everything that you have in your life, even if it is not as fancy as what everyone else has. Often times we forget just how lucky we are to have a roof over our heads, food on our table and clothes on our back. Instead, we get caught up in comparing our roof, food, and clothes to that of everyone else around us. Instead, take time every day to remind yourself of the things in your life that you are grateful for.

5. **Take the time to learn something new every day.** Okay, so most of us do not have time to learn something new every single day, at least not if we want to learn it well, but we can make the time to

learn something new at least once a week. Learn something that is interesting to you, but don't be afraid to step outside of your comfort zone and learn something that is completely new to you.
If you don't know how to cook, learn how to make a new recipe each week, or learn how to crochet, build something or create a painting.

Practice gratitude. Be grateful for everything that you have in your life, even if it is not as fancy as what everyone else has. Often times we forget just how lucky we are to have a roof over our heads, food on our table and clothes on our back.

Instead, we get caught up in comparing our roof, food, and clothes to that of everyone else around us. Instead, take time every day to remind yourself of the things in your life that you are grateful for.

6. **Do something nice for you. Often times, we forget to treat ourselves with the same courtesy that we do other people.** Don't forget to buy yourself an outfit, take yourself out to eat. Remember that you are important too, and you

deserve to be treated as such. You don't always have to put other people before yourself.

7. **Get out.** You don't have to stay cooped up in the house all day. Get out and take a walk, sit in the sunshine, breathe the fresh air or go hang out in the park. It is so easy to forget that there is life outside the walls of our homes, to forget how great it feels to leave the house and even how great it can feel to finally come home. If you are struggling with your self-esteem and find that it is because you are stuck in the house all of the time, start making some changes that will allow you to get out more. You may even decide that a part-time job outside of the home is the answer… even if you are running a full-time business from your home.

8. **Surround yourself with supportive people who uplift you instead of tear you down.** These types of people do exist, however; you may find that they are hard to find. Once you become a supportive and uplifting person you will find that these people are attracted to you. Create a weekly group where you get together with like-minded people, sharing your thoughts, experiences and feelings.

9. **Stop judging yourself.** Stop judging your feelings or thinking that you should not feel that way that you do. If you are a sensitive person allow yourself to be a sensitive person. Do not feel guilty for being who you are. Embrace who you are, explore who you are and stop resisting being yourself.

10. **Get rid of the technology and just be.** You have to spend some time disconnected. You do not always have to be connected, you do not always have to know what is going on with every person in your life. Sometimes you just need to shut all of the technology down and just be. Go sit by the edge of a lake, hang out under a tree in your front yard and just exist. Do not think about anything but instead, focus on the world that is around you.

There are so many ways for you to improve your self-esteem and these are just a few of the best tips. By using these tips, you are going to put yourself on the road to improving your self-esteem.

Chapter 9- Creating an environment that boosts self-esteem

Your environment has a lot to do with the way that you feel about yourself. I stated in previous chapters that if you are living in a dirty environment that you will struggle with self-esteem. That is why I feel it is important for you to spend some time focusing on your environment.

Begin by choosing a room to start with. If a room is too much for you to handle, begin by choosing a corner of a room or a drawer in a room. Find an area to start, and then gather some supplies. You will need a box, a bowl of soapy water, a cardboard box, a dry towel and a trash bag. Begin by going through your items. You are going to separate them into three categories which will be kept, discard and sell.

The trash items will go in the trash bag, the sale items will go in the cardboard box and the keep items are going to go to a home. Every item that you keep needs to have a home. It needs to have a place that it belongs, a place for it to be all of the time.

As you go through the items of your home, you need to ask yourself a few questions. Ask first, if this is an item that you will use. Then ask if it is an item that you need and finally ask if this is an item that you love. If the answer to any of these questions is yes, then you will keep the item. On the other hand, if the answer to these questions is no, then you do not need the item.

If you decide that you are not going to keep the item, then you will need to ask yourself another question. Does the item have any value? Is the item resalable? If you think that another person might be interested in purchasing the item, wash the item in the bowl of water, dry it off and place it in the cardboard box.

On the other hand, if the item is not salable, toss it into the trash bag. If you decide that you want to keep the item you will wash it in the bowl of water, dry it and place it wherever you decide it will stay.

Make sure that you go through everything in your home. Go through knickknacks, papers, and so forth but don't just stop there. Make sure that you go through your closet, your kid's toys and even the junk drawers.

When you have the entire house done, move on to other areas of your life. Clean up your email. Begin by going through your email and unsubscribing to all of the emails that you do not read on a regular basis. This may take some time if you have subscribed to a lot of junk email lists. If you find that it is taking a long time for you to clean up your email, you may decide that you want to unsubscribe to 10 email lists per day until you are no longer getting junk mail in your inbox.

You can also clean up your social media. There is no reason for you to have 600 friends, especially if you do not know them all. Delete all of those people who just take up your time or send you game requests all day long. You might also want to get rid of all of those negative people as well.

While talking about getting your home organized we should talk about getting your life organized as well. **I have talked a little bit about creating a daily schedule or plan. It is important for you to know each day what you need to get done and to have a list to guide you ensuring you are getting it done.**

You can also create a meal plan and a grocery list. When you create a meal plan, you know exactly what you will be making for dinner each night so that when dinner time comes you are not standing in front of the fridge unsure of what you are going to make.

Knowing what you are going to make just makes life easier. When you create your meal plan, you can create a grocery list, and make sure that you actually take it to the store with you. This will ensure that you have everything to create the meals that you want to make throughout the week without having to worry about going back to the store.

You may be wondering what this has to do with self-esteem but I can tell you from personal experience, <u>that if you are prepared, you are going to feel a lot better about yourself.</u>

If you find that lists work well for you, create lists for every area of your life. This will ensure that you are completely organized and prepared for whatever you need to do.

However, you do need to make sure that you do not become so rigid that you cannot deviate from your lists. Life happens and you have to plan for that. This is why it is important for you to never put tasks off until the last moment.

Chapter 10- Always improving

One of the best ways for you to improve your self-esteem is to ensure that you are always improving. Every day when I wake up, I tell myself that I am going to do better than I did the day before. I am going to do more; **I am going to be faster or I am simply going to be a better person than I was yesterday.**

It is my goal to always improve and that should be your goal as well. Choose one area of your life that you want to improve each week and focus on it. The following week, add another area. If you find that this becomes overwhelming, add another area each month when you are sure that previous changes have stuck.

Begin with the area that you are having the most problems with, create goals and when you meet these goals, give yourself a reward.

<u>No one should ever remain the same as days go by. Instead, they should continue to grow</u>

<u>and improve.</u> When you look back on your life a year from now, it is important for you to see that you have made changes, that you have improved that is one of the best ways for you to improve your self-esteem.

What you do not want to do is to look back on your life and see that you have regressed in your life. It is also important for us to always improve because sometimes when we find that we are not happy with the life that we are living, we begin wishing that we had a different life. **When we focus on improving the life that we do have, we can create the life that we want.**

The great news is that you can create any life that you want and when you spend time improving each day, you will be building that life. Sit down and imagine what your perfect life would look like. What would make you happy? Start working toward that. Start creating a plan that will give you the life that you want.

Imagine a life tomorrow that is better than the life that you lived today. Imagine being more productive tomorrow than you were today and going to bed feeling better about who you are tomorrow than you do tonight.

Imagine doing that every day for a year or five years or even ten years. Imagine how wonderful you will feel waking up every day knowing that it is going to be better than the day before.

Spend time improving upon what is on the inside, your personality, your attitude and what you will find is that the outside improves on its own. Be a kind person, plan to help at least one person every day and not expect anything in return, **but make sure that you are not causing yourself harm by helping others.**

No one should ever remain the same as days go by. Instead, they should continue to grow and improve.

When you look back on your life a year from now, it is important for you to see that you have made changes, that you have improved that is one of the best ways for you to improve your self-esteem.

This is what someone with low self-esteem would do, take from themselves, and give to others what they really need themselves. **Of course, it feels good to help those that are in need but not at the cost of our own happiness.**

Work to be a better parent than you were yesterday, a better housekeeper, a better parent, a better employee and so on. When you focus on doing better in every area of your life, you will find that soon you feel so good about yourself and the person that you have become that you have always wanted to be.

The truth is, those that have high self-esteem, have it because they have accomplished what they have set their minds to, they have spent time improving their life every day in order to create the life that they want.

Conclusion-

Your self-esteem will affect every area of your life, but the great news is that it is in your control. Right now you need to make the choice to take control of your life and your self-esteem. When you take control of your self-esteem and choose to improve it, you will be taking control of your life and creating the life that you want to live.

When people have high self-esteem, they feel good about who they are. They look good and they are productive people. They care about who they are, about their life and they take care of themselves. They also know how to make good decisions.

The only thing that you have to be careful of when you are improving your self-esteem is that you do not improve it so much that you have overly high self-esteem. **It is important to be humble and not think that you are perfect, but it is also important to feel good about yourself. The most important part is for you to find a good balance between the two.**

Did you enjoy reading this book?

Can I ask you a favour?

Thanks for purchasing and reading this book, I really hope you find it helpful.

If you find this book helpful, **please help others find this book by kindly leaving a review.** I love getting feedback from my customers, loved it or hated it! Just Let me know. and I would really appreciate your thoughts.

Thanks in advance

Jennifer N. Smith

This book will help you realize that the only thing that's holding you back from having a better life is YOU! **You had the key to turn your life around.** By reading this book you will become empowered to take charge of your life and stop playing victim to life's seemingly impossible challenges.

This book mentioned about mindfulness and meditation.

If you want to learn more about how to practice mindfulness and meditation, I highly recommend that you check out my meditation book here.

ABOUT THE AUTHOR

For me, the hardest part of being a mom is learning how to manage my own emotions. After having a baby, I found myself yelling at my husband and my son every day, I felt horrible and guilty afterward, and I felt so stressed and tired all the time.

I started reading lots of self-help books and I have learned a lot. Now, I feel happier and positive.

I want to share what I have learned throughout the years with my readers; I hope my books can help you deal with your day-to-day challenges, and make you feel happy again, you can create a home full of peace and love for the whole family.

Printed in Great Britain
by Amazon